MANDY SWIFTSON

VOICE OF A DAMAGED SOUL

Powerful verses of pain.

This is for everyone out there who can relate to any or all of these verses.
This book goes out to you.
This is for the people who didn't manage to heal, those no longer with us, either
from their own hand or from someone else's.
This is also to those who make it their lives mission to help people heal, without
you all the world would be a much more damaged place to be for a lot of people.
No-one deserves to be treated in any of the ways these verses depict.
Stay strong.
Love yourself.
xx

When bad things happen, our soul bleeds.

It hurts, it gets damaged.

Sometimes we turn to destructive ways to try and compensate.

Sometimes we hurt ourselves.

Cuts to the soul may not be visible but they run deep.

Mandy Swiftson 2021

Contents

Foreword

This book came about in the third UK lockdown during the Covid pandemic.

It is very much from a place of pain, however I wasn't in that place when I wrote this.

Which scared a few people close to me beacuse reading the verses they believed I was in a dark scary place.

I have been in that dark scary place many mnay times but thankfully now I am not and I have no intention of allowing myself to become that bad again.

I have the physical and the emotional scars to prove whree I have been, which help me to not want to go back.

-Mandy Swiftson April 2021

Preface

This was very much a soul cleansing and soul repairing piece of work for myself, although I am not convinced those closest to me felt the same as I know a lot of them thought I was talking about now.

I wasn't, I am in a good place (mostly) with thought of darkness in my head.

I do not allow the black dog to rule over me although he does still like to make his unwelcome presence known every so often.

But all of these verses are real. They are times when I felt my soul was broken, I wanted to call this book "Voices of a broken soul" but my husband said it was too dark.

I am not convinced he was right.

When bad things happen to us, abuse, rape, death of a loved one, bullying (the list literally is endless), our soul takes a hit.

Deep down part of us breaks, not necessarily beyond repair but breaks all the same.

Sometimes it is hard to put into words just how bad we feel.

This is what I have tried to do in these verses.

I have tried to get out how bad we feel when our soul takes a hit.

People talk about our hearts all the time, but not our soul.

I am hoping that even if these verses connect with just one person then I have been successful.

Acknowledgement

I need to make some special people aware of how much their support means to me.

__Debz__, for wanting to love every piece of my writing even if the subject is too hard.

__Victoria__ and *__Jordan__*, for reading what I send when I send it and answering too.

__Kirstie__, For supporting me even though some of these were just too much read.

__Charlene__, You know and I know no-one can put the world to rights like we can. (especially if there is a body involved)

__Leighanne__, am sorry for making you believe I was in a such a dark place you considered breaking lockdown rules to check on me. But I love you for worrying.

__Jo,__ My bestest bint in a suit. Always has been and always will be.

__Dude__, For loving me despite me being me and supporting me all the way. Love you dude, always have always will.

And finally you guys, *__my readers__*, without you this crazy journey I am on would not be possible. Whether this is the first or third of my books you have read thank you.

1

WE PLAYED A GAME JUST ME AND HIM.

I don't like the game
He wants me to play
I don't like it at night
I don't like it in the day.

I didn't like it the first time
When he said he loved me
Even when he said I was special
I didn't like it you see!

I didn't know what it was
That the game was called
But I knew what he did
Made me feel appalled.

I told him I didn't
Want to play his game
I told him I would tell
My mum his name.

He told me if I told

Any one what we did
He told me no one would believe me
I mean I was just a kid!

He told me they would make
Me go so very far away
If I ever told another soul
Of the game he liked to play.

What did I know,
I thought what he said was true
So I kept it to myself
What he liked to do.

So I would try so hard
To avoid him at all cost
But when you live in the same house
That battle is already lost.

The monster you see
Is not under the bed
Or in the cupboard
Or even in my head.

The monster in my house
Is very real and alive
So now I try and figure out
How I am going to survive.

I can't tell anyone my secret
I have no-one with to share
It is my secret to keep to myself
My cross for only me to bear.

WE PLAYED A GAME JUST ME AND HIM.

No one would believe me anyway
So who would I dare tell
There is no-one of course
So I just retreat to my shell.

I know I changed from then
Into a different kind of child
I went from filled with fun and laughter
To distant meek and mild.

Nothing I did was ever good enough
Nothing I did was ever right
But what do you expect
With the monster in the night

I didn't like the game
He made me play
I didn't like the game
But what could I say

I was too small just a kid
I didn't make any difference to him
There was nothing I could do
Not even on a whim.

When time to play
Comes about once again
I try and switch off completely
And see if I can get lost in my brain.

I would pretend I was magic
And that I could fly away
To somewhere very magical

Where these games I didn't have to play.

The thing about my magical place
The place where I pretend to be
No one has a special game
Not for any one not even me.

I don't like the game
He wants to play
But I can cope with it better
When I am far away.

I wish I could stay
Forever away
I wish I didn't have
A special game to play.

2

WILL I EVER HEAR THE WORDS MY SOUL NEEDS.

What do I need to do
To hear you say that you are proud?
What do I need to do
To make you say it out loud?

Every time I try to work
That little bit extra hard,
Every time I bring home
An extra mark on a report card.

I am just waiting for the words
I just want to hear you say
I have waited forever
And I hope for them every day.

Every time that I manage
To achieve something new,
The first person I want to share with

Is always you.

I tell myself this time
You will say those words to me,
You will tell me that you are proud
And then everyone would see.

They would see I am something
That I am important too,
They will see I am special
And that I actually mean something to you.

But not today they will not see that
Because I still I did not get to hear,
Those little words that would mean so much
And of course a nice little cheer.

The others they hear it so often
It feels to me like its all the time,
But never for me do you ever say it
That's just feels like such a crime.

You seem not to remember all the time
You actually have three children and not just two
Surely we should all be treated and
Mean exactly the same to you.

But the others don't seem to have to work
For your affection and praise the same way that I do
I just seem to anger, annoy and disappoint
Rather than ever please you.

Why don't you love me?

And treat us all the same
Why is it never for anything good
Whenever you shout my name?

It is always me that is in the wrong
Even if I am not the one to blame
But it doesn't matter when I explain it to you
Because you will always think the same.

You don't ever believe be capable of doing anything right
You do not believe anything that I have to say
The others you believe instantly
But that seems to be just your way.

You tell me that I am a liar
And that I always do things to make you mad
I know that I am no where near perfect
But I do not really think I all bad.

Sometimes I ask you a question
Maybe I ask why or ask how
Your response is always the same to me
And it starts with 'get here now'.

Then you start the yelling in my face
Telling me how stupid I will always be
This is something you never tell the others this
You only feel the need to say it to me.

I don't know what I did at the start
But I must have done something when I was small
For you to treat me in this way
And for the names for me you do call.

I don't know why you won't love me
I don't know why you treat me so tough,
Maybe it was the truth that was said
And without me you had enough.

Maybe I didn't bring anything
To the ready made family of four
Maybe you only wanted two children
And you never ever wanted any more

That would make some sense
As to why I am treated like you do
Nothing I did would ever be enough
But it was never me it was you.

If you didn't want another
If two was perfect for you
Then you should have done something to stop anymore
And keep the number at two.

But that isn't what happened
And two became three
And so you decided it didn't matter
Because I wasn't important, no not me.

You acted like at times
I simply didn't exist
But then you would let me know how you felt
With a slipper, belt or fist.

I am sorry I wasn't special enough
for you to love me too
But you know what that is ok

WILL I EVER HEAR THE WORDS MY SOUL NEEDS.

Because I can say I still loved you.

So when I ask the question this time
I know the answer is not one that can be said
I know the answer in my heart
I know the answer in my head.

What do I need to do
To make you love me too?
What do I need to do
To make you say I am proud of you?

Nothing is the answer
Nothing will get what I need
Nothing will be good enough
I just need to take heed.

3

I FEEL NOTHING. AM I DEAD?

Am I dead?
I ask as I lock the door,
Am I dead?
I ask as I search for more.

Am I dead?
I ask as I get things out,
Am I dead I ask?
I need something with clout.

Am I dead?
I ask as I find what I need,
Am I dead?
I ask ready to plant the seed.

Am I dead?
I ask as the first one takes,
Am I dead?
I ask or is this another mistake?

Am I dead?

I FEEL NOTHING. AM I DEAD?

I ask as I do one more,
Am I dead?
I ask while sat on the floor.

I am not dead!
I say as I feel this pain,
I am not dead!
I say again and again.

I am not dead!
I say as the blood runs free,
I am not dead!
I say to no one but me.

I am not dead!
I say as I count each cut,
I am not dead!
I say as I start on my foot.

I am not dead!
I say I just needed to feel,
I am not dead!
I say but they always heel.

I need the release,
I need to let go,
I need the release,
It is not easy you know.

I need the release,
To let the bad out
I need the release,
It doesn't help to shout.

I need the release,
It's my way to cope,
I need the release,
Surely it's healthier than dope.

I need the release,
I need the control,
I need the release,
I need it for my soul.

Cut cut bleed
This is the pattern that I do,
Cut cut bleed
In places a new.

Cut cut bleed
And I start to feel better,
Cut cut bleed
And the demons don't matter.

Cut cut bleed
And I can let myself be,
Cut cut bleed
And for a while it's just for me.

Cut cut bleed
I can be at peace once again,
Cut cut bleed
Oh I love the pain.

The pain you see I need
For my life to move on,
The pain you see I need

For me to feel like I belong.

The pain you see I need
For anything to be right
The pain you see I need
To help me get through the night.

The pain you see I need
To accept what happened in the past,
The pain you see I need
But the problem is it won't last.

The pain you see I need
To help me get through the day,
The pain you see I need
Has already started to fade away.

Am I dead?
I ask as I lock the door,
Am I dead?
I ask as I sit on the floor.

4

THE TIMELINE.

To start with they will be nice
They will not pick fault,
Probably because they realise
You would quickly bolt.

They won't tell you that you're ugly
Or that you need to get thin,
They won't have a need for competition
That they always must win.

Little comments is how it always starts
when it begins to take place,
Nothing to major or big
still Not invading your personal space.

Wear this instead, they may say to you
Please do not wear that,
I like you in this, much better
And you don't want to look too fat.

How nice is that, you think at first

That they want you to feel good,
Treating you nice and kindly
Like any good partner would.

This will carry on I guess
for a short amount of time
Nothing to serious or major
And still nowhere near a crime.

The helpful remarks they once made
Soon begin turn to something more,
They start the nit picking and moaning
And so your insecurities will begin to soar.

First they comment on what you are wearing
Then maybe the way you look too,
Negative comments, constantly coming you way
All said with the aim of belittling you.

You are lucky, they will say
To have me in your life,
No one else would want you
Their explanation cuts you like a knife.

Next they will start to say
Where you can and cannot go,
Every time you touch your phone
What you are doing they will want to know.

In time they will make sure you
Lose all contact will all,
They want you to have No one to turn too
They want you to have no one to call.

So now they have you
Dressing as they see fit
And no one to talk too
Or with to just chat and sit.

you see Little by little
your life and control they have took
But still they will want to tell you
You still have so much luck.

No one will love you they say
As much as what they do,
No one will treat you like this
They will make you believe it's true.

So you try to do as you are told
Because you are on your own
You have no supporters and family around
And all your friends the nest they have flown.

Next along comes the rules
The right way and the wrong,
Listen to them carefully they say
Or the lesson will be very long.

Then one day, one of the rules
You will accidentally break,
The punishment now they say
you will have to take.

A slap maybe or a punch
Or possibly a kick,
Just once or twice this first time

THE TIMELINE.

It will be over really quick.

So, you are sat in shock,
That they did this to you
What will happen next?
What should you do?

But then they say they are sorry
They promise It won't happen once more,
I love you, please forgive me they plead
I promise to love you from my core.

Confusion is what you feel now
As to what you must do,
They are sorry and upset
And of course they love you.

You see it only happened the once
And you were probably to blame,
So you of course you agree to forgive them
And pretend things are the same.

But they are not the same and will never be so
But you just won't see it yet,
You forgave them that one time
So now your future with them is set.

You see now you have forgiven them this
You have given them the OK,
To treat you as they please
Day after day after day.

It may be another few days

Or you may even make a week,
But soon they will determine
More Punishment you do seek.

And so another good hiding
For what you apparently did wrong
You clearly didn't do as you were told
Or you just spoke for too long.

So some slaps and some punches
Some dragging you by your hair,
If you get Marks and bruises, no worries
You see now they just don't care.

I mean no one will see you with them
Because remember You are all alone
You won't be going anywhere anyway
And oh yeah they have already taken your phone.

So From now on the punishments you need
Will be happening all the more,
They will be pushing you out of their way
They will be throwing you to the floor.

You won't have any control now
Not Of anything you do,
They will decide everything that happens
None of it will be you.

They will decide What you eat and when you sleep
They will decide if you can watch on TV,
You don't get to decide anything
Not even what you have to cook for their tea.

The depth of pain you are in
Doesn't seem to even register anymore
You can't tell them the broken bone is hurting
Or that new black eye is sore.

So this is your life now so you just carry on
With Good hidings happening day after day
You keep try to watch what you are doing
And keep monitoring the things that you say.

Every day you try so hard
To remember each new rule,
You try and see the good in it all
Like pretending you are at school.

But today you know what is coming
Because you have seen that look before,
So maybe you should just get it over with
And deliberately annoy them some more.

Because you know from experience what happens
When they sit and stew,
You know the resulting punishment
Will ten times worse for you.

So yeah you do something on purpose
To break make sure you break the camel's back,
And then here it comes quickly
The very first waited for whack.

You can almost feel happy now
That this punishment has begun,
Because you know when it over

Their sour mood will be done.

It's actually crazy to think about
How your life before used to be,
No restrictions on the places you could visit
No restrictions on the people you could see.

But you know this is your lot now
This is the only life you deserve,
You are only there to be their punch bag
And all their needs to serve.

But what about if we just go back
To look where things went wrong,
Looking back now it's easy
Like the words of well-loved song.

That first time you forgave them
Was when you made the mistake,
When really you should have
Allowed this to make your senses wake.

There should be no sorry for this happening
There should be no need to forgive
You should have said to them
Get lost for this is my life to live.

One time is not acceptable
One time should not go passed
If it does happen you should be saying
That one time was the last.

Never let them tell you

That to be with them is good luck
Because let's face it in all honesty
That person really does just suck.

You see my dear are better
And deserve much more than all of that,
Don't ever let your partner
Convince you that your fat.

So you see have respect yourself
And be happy with who you are
Because then when someone criticises
You can send them afar.

Don't let them take your control
Because you are just give them the power.
Don't let them tell you which is better to have
Whether it be A bath or a shower.

No partner ever has the right
To call you a hurtful name,
Do not allow them to carry on
Do not let them make you feel shame.

Tell them this is not acceptable
Not even just one time,
Tell them you are reporting them
Tell them it's an awful crime.

Domestic abuse is not clever
Domestic violence is not good,
Everyone deserves to be treated
How a special loved one should.

So If you are in a situation
Where the above is happening now,
There is help out there available
To help you escape somehow.

Please don't suffer this horror any more
You have already been through enough
I can guarantee they will not like it
But simply put that is tough.

So please make sure you love yourself
And make sure you are always treated with care
Please feel free to read this
And please feel free to share.

5

THE LIVING BLACK DOG

Some people call me a dark cloud,
To others I am the black dog.
Some simply call me depression
And to others I am like a fog.

It doesn't matter to me,
What name to me you give,
It only matters to me,
That you help to make me live.

People will ask you
"why are you sad?"
And when you can't answer
They just get mad.

"Get over it!" they say
"There is simply no need"
But I am here to tell you
I won't let you succeed.

You see I am real

And I will fight you every day,
I know you have your demons
And you need to keep them at bay.

But the thing about me
I know what they are
So I will use them
Over and again to push you so far.

I will plant a seed or idea
In your broken mind
I will tell you that you are horrible
That you are also unkind.

I will use different words
To make you feel low
I will make you doubt who you are
And everything you know.

I know some days you will beat me
And I will not be around
But we both know it's only temporary
For me and you are bound.

Yes you will beat me
For months or even years,
But then something will happen
And I will feed from your tears.

There will be days
When I make you want to stay in bed
These are the days
When I am right in your head.

When you are sad I am happy
When you are weak I am strong
I will fight you tooth and nail
All your life long.

You see I am the black dog
And disappear I do not
I may just be hiding
And not seen a lot.

Whilst you may not be seeing me
Someone else wont be so good
I will be messing with their heads
Just like a good black dog should.

So listen to me you doubters
Those who tell them to smile
They can smile all they want
But I will chase them mile for mile.

Don't doubt the strength I carry
Over your loved ones mind
Don't doubt I will win
I am one of a kind.

Some call me a dark cloud
Some call me the black dog
Some simply call me depression
But you too could get lost in my fog.

6

I SAID NO.

I said no! I explain to them once more,
I thought no means no.
I said no I repeat my self once again,
No does not mean let's go.

Yes I had a drink with him
But I still said no!
Yes I had a dance with him
I maybe put on a show,

Yes we left together
But I still said no,
Yes we went for a walk
It was a nice night, so,

Yes I know we shared a kiss
But that doesn't mean I wanted more,
So I made sure I told him no
As he pushed me to the floor.

Yes I had had a few drinks

But I still knew no!
I didn't want sex
And I made sure I let him know

I struggled to make him get off me
But I still kept telling him no!
He told me he knew I wanted it
But I still said kept on saying no!

I tried so hard to fight him off
I tried to get myself free
I wanted to scream and shout for help
But his hand across my mouth stopped me

'I brought you a drink' he sneered
'You at least owe me this'
'You led me on' he said
'You were saying yes with that kiss'.

I didn't I scream but only I hear it inside
This is not what I am about,
I wanted him to get off of me
I wanted to to be able to shout.

'I don't care!' he told me
'That you said no!'
'Fight me all you like'
'It won't make any difference you know'.

'In fact,' he said
With an evil look
'Carry on with your fighting it makes me harder'
'And makes me really just want to fuck'

In my head I am screaming loudly
No no NO please stop!
I can feel his hands on my trousers
On the button at the top.

His hands are moving lower
Now they are inside me
I keep my eyes closed tightly
I can't bear to open them and see.

I feel sick I do, and I actually want to die
As he pulls his trousers low
Stop don't do this to me I plead in my head
You know I told you no.

He didn't listen he didn't care
He took what wasn't his to take
I hoped it would be over quickly
For my own sanity's sake.

I don't know how long he took
To make himself cum
I don't know how long I laid there
After he finished because I was numb

Seconds maybe minutes or maybe hours
The time seemed to stand still
After he left me there bleeding
After he took his fill.

Someone came across me
They took me some place
For medical attention

I SAID NO.

And an inquisition I had to face.

Who did this to you?
What is his name? Are you sure?
Did you wear that outfit on purpose
To make yourself a lure?

What difference does it make
If my top went low
What difference does it make
When I said no!

Are you sure you said no
And you didn't just change your mind?
Are you sure you didn't want this
As is usual for your kind?

Listen to me please
I cry out to them once more
I didn't want to have sex with him
In the park on the floor

Yes I to him no!
Yes I made myself very clear
I told him no again
And he just responded with a sneer

I didn't offer what he wanted
I didn't give him what he took
I just wanted to enjoy myself
I wasn't looking for a quick fuck

I want to press charges

I want this animal caught
I didn't go out looking for this
This isn't what I sought.

I am sobbing freely now
I want it all to go away
I want to be someplace I can shower
And scrub the memories away

They finally leave me alone
I think I Have made them understand
I feel like my life is now over
Like I am already sinking in quick sand

I turn the water on
I make sure it is too hot
I scrub and scrub and scrub again
But feel clean I do not.

The water in the shower
Had turned from hot to cold
I still sit there freezing
I feel like I have been sold.

My life right now is nothing
After what that man took from me
I am going to get out now
And have a drink or maybe three.

I open the bottle I find
I swig it straight from there
It actually burns my throat so bad
I actually don't even care.

I SAID NO.

I drink and drink
Then I drink some more
I want to forget everything
I want that down to my core

I need to forget forever
What he took but I didn't give
How do I forget this?
How can I still live?

He took more than sex from me
When he raped me that night
He took away my happiness
He took away my light.

I don't go out now
I don't socialise any more
I won't leave the safety of my home
I wont venture out my door.

I said no! I know I did
And I said it lots of times
I said no! to that monster
As he committed those crimes.

My best friend now is a bottle
I use it to help me get some sleep
The memories of me dying
I have buried so deep

That is what it has felt like
That was the death of me
I am now locked up in a box

And that rapist has the key

I don't want to give him my life
I don't want to let him win
I don't want to exist like this
But I am scared to let anyone in

I do not want to talk about it
I don't want to relive it again
That's why I use the bottle
So I can hide from all my pain.

I have got to go to court they said
I have to tell everyone what he did
I have to sit and face my attacker
No chance who am I trying to kid

I know I cannot do it
I can't look in his eye
If I ever have to see him again
I think I will actually die

Then they tell me
I can tell my tale from behind a screen
I don't actually have to look at him
And be reminded of just how he is mean.

So I am sat here now behind a screen
Telling all of what he did do
I answer question after question
And when they say I put it to you

Even though I am shaking badly

I SAID NO.

Even though I want out
I tell them what happened
And how NO is what I did shout

I tell them how he shoved me
Down on to the floor
I tell them how he used his hands
Them how he used more

I told them he raped me
I said the words so clear
I told them all I had wanted
Was to join him for a beer.

Finally the jury go out
Innocent or guilty which way will they go
Did she really want this
Or did she really say no

If she said no it is definitely rape
No matter what he did claim
If she said no repeatedly
There is no one but him to blame

They eventually come back
Have you decided? the judge asks them
What is your verdict
Freedom or to condemn

Guilty! the foreman says
With conviction in his word
Did I hear them correctly
Or have I mis heard

No I heard them right
As they declared his fate
Thankfully it wasn't that long
Before his sentence we had to wait.

I think he should have gotten longer
I think the sentence was too lame
But everyone knows what he did
Everyone now knows his name.

I have now decided the bottle
Will not be emptied in MY glass
I am taking my life in my hands again
And seeking help at last

He took from me what I didn't give
He took what wasn't his to take
But I have to make myself get better now
For mine not his sake

I refuse for him to haunt me
From now until I die
I refuse to let him take my life
With the evil in his eye

I was raped by a monster
But he did not break my soul
You see I am a survivor
And I have re made myself whole.

7

THE PERSONAL PAIN.

When you lose someone you love
The word grief can mean so much
From tears and heartbreak
To anger and such

No-one can tell you
How you should or shouldn't behave
No one has the right
To tell you that you need to be brave.

Alone and scared and frightened
Lost and confused and afraid
These are some of the emotions
Through which you must wade.

Five stages of grief they say
You must fight through
Before the life you want to live
Will give any form of peace for you.

The first stage they say of grief

A strong denial it will be
You won't believe any of it is true
And real proof you will need to see.

No you say, no just no
This simply cannot be right
You will keep on denying day after day
You will keep denying through the night.

The second stage apparently
Is when the anger starts to come through
Your rage at the world grows daily
You may curse fate something new.

Pissed off with the world and all
How dare this be right
It wasn't time for your person
To travel into the light.

Bargaining is the next stage you will pass
In your attempt to make things clear
You say I promise I will do this or that
Just please keep them close and near

You will offer up your soul to the devil
Your life in exchange for the one you lost
You will offer up your last penny if you can
You will offer whatever the cost.

The fourth stage is next and this is the toughest
You see Depression is this one
You feel like you can't cope anymore
Because an evil force has won.

You don't feel there is much point to life
Your life feels empty and defunct
You hopes and dreams are over
Your balloon has burst and your ship has sunk.

Acceptance is the last stage of grief
To fight through in your own way
This is when you know for certain
You have your goodbyes to say.

You know for sure 100%
They are not ever coming back
They are gone from earth forever
That you now know is a cold hard fact.

But what they don't tell you when you grieve
What's not written in the rules
Are the things you worry and stress about
And how people treat you like fools

They think you are not capable
Of making decisions on your own
But they don't want to listen to you
Cry and grieve and moan

You see grief is very much I'm afraid
A private cross to bear
Even with people around you
That you know do actually care.

No one knows how much you hurt
Or the things that you feel
No one can say what is right or wrong

Or even what is real

What no one ever tells you
Is of the hurt that goes so deep
Nothing you have ever felt before
Nothing you will want to keep

You see its not like a headache
Where you can simply take a pill
Or even like sprain to the ankle
Where you can just chill.

Emotional pain is so much worse
And cuts you deep like a knife
This pain will bury itself deep inside of you
And be present for the rest of your life.

They same times heels everything
And makes the pain go away
But actually its not that
You just cope better day by day.

When it is raw in the beginning
And nothing seems alright
When you spend your days crying
And there is no sleeping at night

The pain is so unbearable
Is so hard to cope
You don't have the will for much at all
Its easier to just mope.

But I promise over time

THE PERSONAL PAIN.

You will cry less and less
The days will feel a bit brighter
You won't feel such a mess

One day maybe after a month
Maybe not till after a year
You will find you first reaction
Is a smile and not a tear.

This doesn't mean you stop hurting
Or missing the one who you have lost
Its just natures way of dealing
Like when a thaw follows a frost

Grief is such a powerful thing
But it doesn't beat natures true force
So day by day and step by step
Just let it run its course.

Don't try to fight it
Don't let it win
Don't stop plodding forward
Don't ever give in

One or two or three years from now
You will remember them with a smile
A smile so bright and beautiful
You could light the darkest mile.

The tears won't last forever
You won't always feel so sad
One day in the future you will wake
And suddenly life won't seam so bad

But when you lose someone you love
Your grief is yours to get through
No one can suffer it instead
This one is just for you.

8

WOULD LIFE BE BETTER IF I WERE DEAD?

I don't think I can carry on anymore
With fighting this life
When every breath I take
Cuts me deep like a knife.

I just don't think
I want to breathe any more
Every breath is so hard
It makes my heart sore

I think the world would be a better place
For everyone if I was just gone
No more worry for everyone anymore
It would all be just done.

I won't have to be hurting
My heart can be free
They won't have to stress and worry
Anymore about me

I think it would be easy
To make that call
To make my life over
Once and for all

There are many different routes
I can choose to take
So I guess right now
I have a decision to make

I could take some tablets
I know I would need a lot
But tablets are messy
And guaranteed they are not

So I could slit my wrists
With a sharp sharp knife
But longways is the way to cut
When you want to end your life

I am not sure I could deal with
The blood and the pain
And if I fail then suddenly
I am back where I was again

By taking a Walk into traffic
Is another way I could go
Or maybe even jumping from a bridge
That would work well you know

There is a few more ways
For me to think about and explore
I can hang a noose from a high beam

So my feet don't touch the floor

I don't think that would be easy
It would definitely not be pain free
I am not sure that is the right
Way to end this life for me

What about a gun fired
A clean shot through the head
One thing is for certain
I would definitely be dead

I don't want to live this life I lead
I just want to be pain free
Everyone would be better off
Without the fuck up that is me

I am definitely going to do this
My death I just need to plan
I want this to be over
In the quickest way I can

I don't want to hurt anymore
I want to be at rest
I know they will all be sad at first
But it really is for the best

I am a total fucking screwup
That they constantly have to deal with
This is why its better
That I choose simply not to live.

Now that I have decided

Now I know what I shall do
Now I know the problems I cause
Will soon be over for you

I am starting to see things clearer
I am starting to see a light
The peace I have been searching for
Will be coming for me tonight.

A see a beautiful rainbow
I want to visit the other side
I am sorry for all the hurt I caused
For the trouble and times I have lied

Please don't blame yourselves
This one is one is as always down to me
But now there will be no more
We will all now be free.

Goodbye to the ones that I love
That will now be in a better place
Now you will be happier
And not have to deal with my face.

Its bright this side of the rainbow
I feel I can just rest
Am sorry to everyone that knew me
But this really was for the best.

9

IS HE CHEATING OR AM I MAD?

Did I smell perfume
Today when a kiss we did share?
But it isn't the perfume
That I usually wear!

It was just a whiff
So I could be wrong
I mean we weren't stood together
Or close for that long.

Is that a new shirt
I haven't seen before?
Check you out, I laugh
Looking after yourself more

It has not been a thing
You have ever bothered to do
Buying different clothes
And trying something new.

That is something else

That I think is new
Taking your phone everywhere
Even when you go to the loo

You never really bothered
Much about your phone before
In fact you said you hated it
And found having one a bore.

Another late meeting
That is the third this week
I jokingly ask
Is there someone else you seek?

"Don't be daft!" you say
"You know that is not true"
You know the only life I want
Is here with the kids and you.

I didn't actually mean it it was just a joke
But now your reaction has made me think
So I am going to go over everything I have noticed
While I ponder over a drink

There have definitely been times lately
When I go to snuggle up to you tight
And you turn away and say to me
"Sorry love! not in the mood tonight"

So am I looking at things
That really are not there?
Or is there something going on
And do I actually care?

Perfume that is not mine
The first thing that comes to mind
Then the new outfits
Of a different kind

Habits that are different
Work days that are long
Everything is adding up
But I still could be wrong

Maybe I should confront you
And ask you straight outright
But do I have the energy
To start the following fight?

If you are cheating on me
I don't know what I will do
What would be my plan for life
And how would I cope without you?

I think maybe I am making
A mountain out of a mole hill
Maybe you are right again
And maybe I should take another pill

You tell me that I am paranoid
You told the doctor I am not well
My mental health is your biggest concern
The worried doctor you do tell.

So now I don't know
What is real and what is not
Maybe I am imagining it

All of it the lot.

But I don't think I am wrong
When I see what I think
Is that lipstick that is
On your shirt in the sink?

So am I crazy stupid
Or am I actually right?
Are you tying to trick me
With all your might?

I am taking my meds precisely
As the doctor told me to
The doctor you see I do trust
But not so much trust for you.

So did I smell perfume
Today when a kiss we did share?
Did I smell perfume
Different to what I would wear?

10

HOW CAN YOU LOVE ME WHEN I DO NOT LOVE ME?

When I look in the mirror
I don't like what I see
I look in the mirror
And wonder how you can love me!

When I see how I have changed
From the woman you wed
I know I am so different
It doesn't need to be said

Back then I was slim
And had nice curves
Now I am so fat
It is just beyond absurd.

I felt so beautiful
On our wedding day
You told me I was too
My princess you would say

I get why you don't
Say the same things now
I mean look at how I look
Why would you? How?

I feel fat I feel ugly
I feel broken too
I don't think I am beautiful anymore
So why would you?

I guess it makes sense
How our intimacy is less
Why would you want to be intimate
When I look such a mess?

Maybe one day at some point
I will feel beautiful once more
And the heat between us
Will once again soar

But for now I guess
I will settle as things are
With loving you and wanting you
From what feels like afar.

11

I DO NOT KNOW WHERE MY PLACE IN LIFE IS.

When suddenly you lose
A job to which you have given your all
It feels very similar
To when you take a fall,

You are suddenly not sure
Of where is your place
Or of where you fit in
Through time and space.

You feel a bit lost
No sure what to do now
Not sure of your next step
Or even of how,

Where do you go next in life
What will be your new working role
Its so hard to focus and find something new
When you have already given your heart and soul.

They tell you its not because of the work you did
But because of a budget cut
They tell you they are sorry
They say they will miss you, but

This doesn't stop you thinking
You are somehow to blame
It doesn't stop you feeling bad
And having feelings of shame.

You were that job that job was yours
You always went above and beyond
You liked the things you needed to do
And of the job role you grew fond.

So you worked so hard
For quite a few years
With lots of blood, sweat and swearing
And you shed many a tears.

So yes now you have lost
What you thought defined you
And now you have go out
And try and find something new.

So you are feeling rather rubbish
With yourself on the whole
And yet you have to go out into the world
And get yourself sold?

A new CV you need to sit and write
But where on earth do you begin?
You have to convince these people

That the job you deserve to win.

But its been so long
Since you were in the job seeking race
You don't realise now
All the obstacles you will face.

So applying for jobs
Is your daily new thing to do
You check it every hour
Just in case there is something new.

Job after job after job
You read through and apply for
But what you have is not enough
They just want more.

A degree in this or that
Before you are in with a shot
Is there no on the job training any more
Apprenticeships and what not?

Graduates and your age
Another battle for you to fight
It feels like another one
Is just out of your sight

Most of the applications you send
Don't even get a 'no thank you'
So you keep on hoping you will get that yes
And an offer of a job that's new

You actually lose count

Of how many jobs you apply for
But wait there are some new ones now
So you sit and apply for some more

Not getting anywhere
Can send you into a funk
You can feel like you are broken
And your ship has sunk.

But soon one day
An interview you will get
This could be it so pull up your socks
Your future could be set.

But yes when you lose a job
You lose more than just the role
Because of what you put into it
You lose part of your heart and soul.

12

I BROKE MY OWN HEART.

Today my heart got broken
Through I choice I had to make
Today my heart was smashed into pieces
From steps I had no choice but to take.

This morning you all went to school
Just another ordinary day
None of us knew when we said goodbye
Our lives would change this way.

I gave you all a kiss
And told you I loved you all
I told you to have a good day
Nothing unusual at all.

None of us knew at that time
That I lied to you
When I said see you later
This wouldn't come true.

I had to make a decision

I had to break my own heart
The choice to let you go
But this was just the start.

How much you must have all hurt
When I didn't arrive as I should
You must have been so confused and worried
But I did the best I could

You see at that point I knew
That you would be hurt again
And well I didn't want that to happen
So you got emotional not physical pain.

He would have hurt you again
Of this I have no doubt
A fist a foot a weapon too
A slap a kick a clout.

So when he sat there and told me
The truth I must tell
And then carries on speaking
And gave me a huge lie to sell.

He wanted me to tell them
That I was to blame
He wanted me to sit there and confess
And wanted me to share the shame.

I knew I had to make a choice
Our lives would never be the same
I knew you would hurt so much
But I knew I would be to blame.

I BROKE MY OWN HEART.

I told them I didn't want you anymore
I told them I couldn't cope
I told them I was done with it all
Did I mean it? NOPE!

You see I had to make them believe
Because I knew what was to come
I knew that with me you were not safe
So I had to protect you as your mum.

Headlines kept flashing
Right before my eyes
The ones in the magazines
Where a child somehow dies.

I kept thinking what if?
One day it was you guys
All because on that day
I sold them his lies.

So instead of telling them
What he wanted me to say
I decided in that instant
There was another way

So yes I told them
I couldn't cope with you any more
Yes I told them to take you
And not bring you back to my door.

I should have gone with you
I can see that clearly now
But I wasn't worried about me

But protecting you somehow.

You all were what was important
But me I didn't think so much
Your safety had to come first
So you were away from his touch.

So yes I know that I hurt you
And made your life quite tough
I know until you were settled
Your life was really rough.

You were passed from pillar to post
And separated just trying to belong
I know you thought I didn't care
But you couldn't have been more wrong.

You see every single day
That passed since we had to part
I thought of each and every one of you
And I remember you in my heart.

Life was not ever easy for me
When I chose to change our lives
The damage he inflicted regularly
With a fist or foot or knives.

I just needed to write this
So one day you will hopefully see
Although I hurt you massively
It was never about me.

I just needed to get you all safe

I BROKE MY OWN HEART.

Like any good mum should
Letting you go was the hardest thing
But at the time the only thing I felt I could.

One day I hope you wont hate me
For the hurt that I did choose
For the times you thought
That to me you were yesterdays news.

You have never been out of my heart
Never far from my mind
But one thing I am grateful for
Is the amazing parents you did find

They are certainly very special
Your mum and your dad
With them you had a better life
Than with me you would have had.

You see from the way he behaved
When you were there no more
I know that I was right
In what my head I saw.

So I know I made mistakes
And wasn't always right
But getting you all to safety
Was worth the fight.

Some of you I have seen
Some I have spoken to
Some I may never get this chance
Which of course is up to you.

I will never stop hoping
That one day I will see you again
That one day you may say I forgive you
For all the hurt and the pain.

For now my loves I will settle
For life the way it falls
But I will never as long as I live
Stop loving and missing you all.

13

THE BULLIED CHILD.

Today, Today I pray it will be
The day once and for all,
The day I manage to defend myself
From the Bully in the hall!

.

For months and months
I have had the same prayer
For months and months
I have suffered this nightmare.

Let me tell you first
All about me,
Let me explain who I am
So you will then see.

My name doesn't really matter
But for the story I need to say
So for now I will be Fred
And we will leave it that way.

So Fred is me

That's who I am,
But really it could anyone
Like John or Paul or Sam.

I am nothing special
I am not rich or poor
I am a bit on the big side
Just chubby nothing more.

I wear glasses too
Is something else about me,
I like to think I am ok
And I try to be friendly.

So a few months back
Things changed at school,
A new kid started
And he wanted to be cool.

So he started hanging
About with the crew,
You know the ones I mean
That cause trouble for you.

This new kid had to prove
He would fit in with them just fine,
So he made a bee line for me
Whilst standing in the line.

So he comes over
And stands near to where I am at,
Then all of a sudden
He shoves me and calls me fat!

It was over so quick
And no harm done right?
So I ignored that it happened
After all I am not one to fight.

The next time something happened
Was during the P.E lesson of football,
From across the field
Names he stated to call.

The more names he called
The more the crew laughed,
I didn't know what to say
Without someone saying I was daft.

It was just fun
I could almost hear them say,
But I really just wanted
Them to all to go away.

After he name calling
Other things then began,
A trip in the hall maybe
Making me look clumsy where they can.

Fatty and porky
They all called me now,
It became the normal thing
For me to hear from them somehow.

Once fully in with the crew
Things became much worse
A shove here and a punch there

Was how the pain started at first.

Fast forward a few months
To where we are today
Two coats have been stolen
And for other things I have had to pay.

I haven't told anyone
Of my suffering at school,
All because one boy
Wants to be so cool!

I want it to stop,
But I don't know who do to tell
My friends cant do anything
Is what I think as I wait for the bell.

I walk down the hall
Checking who is about
"oh look is fatso"
I then hear them shout.

I try to retreat
Run away again,
But I am just not fast enough
To avoid the pain.

One kicks one punches
One catches my face,
Determined to show me
Where is my place.

"Stop!" I shout

THE BULLIED CHILD.

I can't take this any more
"Just stop!" I shout
Whilst on the floor.

They laugh and jeer
"Why don't you make us?"
Then all of a sudden
I felt a strange buzz.

I stood up and looked
The cool kid right in the eye
"Hit me once more
And I swear you will die!"

He laughed at me
As he looked around,
But he was on his own
None of the crew making a sound.

"As if you could stop me
You are just a great big lump!"
And that's when I did it
I jumped up with a thump.

Straight to the nose
The blood flew wide,
Others that had been bullied looked on in shock
As they all gathered by my side.

The kid who tried to be so cool
Was bleeding down his shirt
He was shocked that he was bleeding
And shocked he had gotten hurt.

"No more names. No more hitting out"
I said as I leaned over him
"It ends now not just for me but for everyone"
I said as I kicked him on a whim.

I turned and I walked away
Just leaving him down there
I was shaking because I felt I had just
Stripped my own soul bare.

The voices around me
They all cheered and they clapped
But I went to the heads office
And told him who I had slapped.

I sat and I told
The whole tale of woe
From when it first started
Till I had just said no.

I told him of the things they had done
The things they had stolen from me,
I told him I left him bleeding
And he was down on one knee.

The head he looked at me
And then quietly he said
I am pleased you came to me with this
After all I am the head.

"We will see what becomes
Of this bully once more,
So please when you leave

THE BULLIED CHILD.

Can you close the door?"

I looked at him
And said "but what of what I did
I mean I have just told you
How I punched and kicked a kid!"

"I know what you said
That you did to that child,
But from what others have said
Compared to what he has done this was mild!

"You see I have had
Other children who have come to me
And tell me of this new kid
But there was no proof and I needed to see.

"So now you have taught him
That in this school
It is much better to be kind
And that makes you cool.

"You see this boy
Will see all your new friends
And I think his bullying
Has now come to an end."

"So no you are not in trouble
This one time is free,
But don't make a habit of it
Or you will be back before me."

I closed the door

As he asked me to
So now I have
A message for you.

Don't go to school
In fear every day
Speak up loud
And have your say.

Tell a teacher, Tell your mum
Tell your friends too
Don't just put up with it
Do what you have to do.

Because bullying is not cool
Bullying is not a good way
Make friends not enemies
Will give you a better day

And Bullies remember before you call someone fat
Or knock their glasses from their head,
Think about the kids that die
By their own hand in their bed.

Think of how much pain
you can make them go through
When they end their life because of it
It will be on you.

Bullying has long term affects
Bullying hurts the heart
The best way to stop this hurt

THE BULLIED CHILD.

Is to make sure it does not start.

If you know of someone being bullied
If you have seen this being carried out,
Don't stand there quiet
Instead stand there and shout.

You see bullies are cowards
Bullies need to stop
They need to know that violence
Wont get them to the top!

So yes today was the day
I finally stood up to the crew,
It wasn't just for me though
Because it was also for you.

14

ONE LITTLE SHOT IS ALL I NEED.

I hurt so bad
I hurt inside
When they asked me if I was ok
I actually lied

I hurt in side
But I want to be OK
So I just tell them
What they want me to say

The pain runs deep
But nothing you can see
This pain is mine
Its just for me

So I am going to have one little shot
To keep the pain at bay
Just one small one
To help me through the day

You see one little shot

ONE LITTLE SHOT IS ALL I NEED.

Helps the pain die down
But I can't tell anyone
As they will frown

But they don't understand
What I feel inside
They don't understand
How I want to hide

One little shot
and my head is clear
One little shot and
The demons I can't hear

One little shot
Soon leads to one more
So just two little shots
To make me soar

Two little shots
Is good for a while
Those two little shots
They help me smile.

But I have had a bad day
It was really rough
So I don't think
Two shots will be enough

So from one to two
And then three four and five
Those little shots
They keep me alive

71

The pain inside
It runs too deep
The shots are struggling
The demons to keep.

So now I have shots
But they are now not small
The shots they shout at me
I just answer their call

So one little shot
To keep the pain at bay
Turned to many a shot
To make it through the day

I don't feel pain with my shots
I just fly free
I don't feel pain with my shots
And I can just be.

But without my shots
However many I take
The pain cuts deep
Make no mistake

One day I hope
I will need no shots
But the thought of how I get there
Leaves me tied in knots

I think they have noticed
That something isn't right
I have tried to hide it

ONE LITTLE SHOT IS ALL I NEED.

I tried with all my might

But they are starting to question
If I am really OK
I have my shots
So yeah I say

They don't believe me
Like they did before
But I can't deal with that now
Where's my shot I need more

My shot doesn't argue
My shot doesn't fight
My shot simply makes
Everything alright.

My shot doesn't question
And ask if I am OK
My shots just keep
The damn pain at bay.

My shot doesn't argue
My shot doesn't fight
My shot simply makes
Everything alright.

EPILOGUE

BROKEN OR DAMAGED

"I am damaged goods
Broken beyond repair"
The first words spoken
As I slumped in the chair,

"A hazz-matt suit
And some toxic waste bins too
Is what you will need to clear my head"
I next said to you,

"There is so much crap
Inside of my head
I am broken beyond repair"
I once again said,

"Not broken but damaged"
You response to me
"That is why you are here
You have hope you see",

"Tell me what made you come
And see me today
Tell me the things you want help with"
I hear you say,

I open my mouth not sure what to say
But then out it all came
I told of my hurts my abuse
And I told you of my shame,

So much came out
With no filters or thought
Everything that had happened
The battles I had fought,

Your face said it all
You didn't know how to process
Everything I was sharing
I was clearly a mess,

Domestic abuse yep that's a tick
Sexual abuse another tick too
Death of a loved one another tick for me
All and more I dumped on you.

I let it all out
I poured out my heart
Now you could see
What I meant at the start,

Clearly you were not expecting
So much to fly from within
But you didn't let it phase you
Just said "Where shall we begin"

"Thank you." You said
"For being honest with me
Thank you for sharing

For helping me see"

"You have suffered the world
You have been to hell and back
I can understand why
You fell off the track"

"What do you want
To explore when we meet?"
"I don't want to self-harm anymore
I want my demons beat"

So we started to talk
Whenever we met
We talked about objectives
And goals were set,

You made me explore
What I had buried away
You made me admit
What I refused to say,

I wanted to hate you
For making me cry
I wanted to blame you
When you tried to pry,

But when I first started
My journey with you
I really believed I was broken
Through and through

But you actually helped me

And made me realise
You made me see things clearly
And open my eyes

I was NOT broken
Beyond any help or repair
I was worth helping
And you did care,

So yes you would pry
And make me admit
You would not let me fall further
And just wallow and sit.

You helped me to see
I was someone of worth
You made me feel like
I had a place on this earth

You worked your magic
Almost like a spell
You got me shouting from the rooftops
And ringing that bell

I am not a piece of crap
On the bottom of anyone's shoe
You gave something back to me
My self-worth all new,

So whilst it was hard
To hash out all my shit
I have no bad feelings towards you
Not even one bit

You took me on a journey
That felt like to hell and back
But what you also did for me
Was to get me on the right track

You gave me little things
To help me to cope
You made sure I have the ways
To get me out of a mope

You showed me healthier ways
To deal other than to self-harm
You taught me to find my inner peace
And to rely on my calm.

Thank you for fixing
For the damage to my soul
Thank you for dragging me
Out of the darkest hole

Not once have I cut
Since I last saw you
Not once have I thought of death
This much is true.

You probably don't realised
You actually saved me
My life is worth living
This you made me see.

About the Author

I am a married lady, on the higher side of 45, I have lived in Nottingham England (Robin Hood Land) all my life apart from a few years where I moved to the posh Harrogate, I am not posh and it didn't work.

I am a bit like Henry V111 but instead of "divorced beheaded died" I have Alcoholic, Psycho and died. So I am a bit of a serial name changer, I am married to hubby number 4 but I know this time I have found my soul mate. He is the fish to my chips, the salt to my vinegar, the yin to my yang. My Dude is my life.

Along with my Dude, there are some other people that keep me going in this crazy world we live in. I don't need to name you because you know who you are.

Writing for me growing up was always something I enjoyed, but the truth is life happened and writing stopped. During the Covid pandemic in 2020 when the whole of the UK was in lockdown for the first time I needed something to stop me feeling utterly useless. So I started to write. "The Mistake" and 9 "Timmy's Magic Book" stories were born.

This came about during the 3rd lockdown in the UK. The words just came when they came, there were times when I was mid conversation with my dude and I would suddenly get my phone out and start writing on my note app. When the words come we don't try and stop them.

You can connect with me on:

f https://www.facebook.com/mandyswiftson

Also by Mandy Swiftson

The Mistake was published in October 2020. It was a very hard book to write. It is a hard book to read and tissues are advised.

Timmy's Magical Treasure Hunt was published in February 2021. It is such fun and the amazing Land Dawson brought the characters to life with her illustartions.

The Mistake

All your life you are taught to forgive. It doesn't matter who or what your beliefs are even as children we are taught we should forgive.

Is forgiveness ever the wrong thing to do?
What if forgiving someone alters your life in ways you could never imagine?

Is it still the right thing to do?
Surely there must be exceptions to the forgive and forget rule?

One forgiveness.
One mistake.
One life altering decision.

Who is right who is wrong?
Forgiveness or survival?

Timmy's Magical Treasure Hunt

Who would like to go on a magical adventure?

Timmy is just a normal little boy with a magical imagination.

Timmy has a very special book, this book takes him on lots of magical adventures.

Join Timmy on a once in a lifetime treasure hunt.

He has clues to follow and he gets to meet new friends and magical creatures.

Timmy is waiting, he is waiting for you to enjoy this magical journey with him.

TO START YOUR ADVENTURE

JUST OPEN YOUR BOOK

TURN THE FIRST PAGE

AND TAKE A LOOK

WHERE WILL IT TAKE YOU?

WHERE WILL YOU BE?

DINOSAURS OR TREASURES?

I CAN'T WAIT TO SEE.